W9-CCU-406

Pebble™ Plus

Healthy Eating with MyPyramid

Being Active

by Mari C. Schuh

Consulting Editor: Gail Saunders-Smith, PhD

Consultant: Barbara J. Rolls, PhD
Guthrie Chair in Nutrition
The Pennsylvania State University
University Park, Pennsylvania

Capstone press
Mankato, Minnesota

Pebble Plus is published by Capstone Press,
151 Good Counsel Drive, P.O. Box 669, Mankato, Minnesota 56002.
www.capstonepub.com

Copyright © 2006 by Capstone Press, a Capstone imprint. All rights reserved.
No part of this publication may be reproduced in whole or in part, or stored in a retrieval system, or
transmitted in any form or by any means, electronic, mechanical, photocopying, recording, or otherwise,
without written permission of the publisher. For information regarding permission, write to Capstone Press,
151 Good Counsel Drive, P.O. Box 669, Dept. R, Mankato, Minnesota 56002.

Books published by Capstone Press are manufactured with paper
containing at least 10 percent post-consumer waste.

Library of Congress Cataloging-in-Publication Data
Schuh, Mari C., 1975–
    Being active / by Mari C. Schuh.
    p. cm.—(Healthy eating with MyPyramid)
    Summary: "Simple text and photographs present the importance of being active and examples of how
to stay active"—Provided by publisher.
    Includes bibliographical references and index.
    ISBN-13: 978-0-7368-5368-2 (hardcover)   ISBN-10: 0-7368-5368-5 (hardcover)
    ISBN-13: 978-0-7368-6921-8 (softcover pbk.)   ISBN-10: 0-7368-6921-2 (softcover pbk.)
    1. Physical fitness for children—Juvenile literature. 2. Exercise for children—Juvenile literature.
I. Title. II. Series.
RJ133.S34 2006
613.7'042—dc22   2005023714

Credits
Jennifer Bergstrom, designer; Kelly Garvin, photo researcher/photo editor

Photo Credits
Capstone Press/Karon Dubke, cover, 3, 9, 22 (swimming, playing catch); Comstock Images, 22 (soccer ball), 7;
Corbis/Ariel Skelley, 11, 19; Corbis/Don Mason, 5; Corbis/George Shelley, 15; Corbis/Tim Pannell, 21; Getty
Images Inc./Alistair Berg, 1; Getty Images Inc./Manzo Niikura, 13; Image Ideas Inc., 22 (soccer); Masterfile/
Masterfile, 17; RubberBall Productions, 22 (jumping rope, in-line skating, dancing, running, and riding bike);
U.S. Department of Agriculture, 8 (inset), 9 (computer screen)

The author dedicates this book to her former physical education teacher, Phil Hanson, and her former track
and cross-country coach, Bob Bonk, both of Fairmont, Minnesota.

**Information in this book supports the U.S. Department of Agriculture's MyPyramid for Kids
food guidance system found at http://www.MyPyramid.gov/kids.**

**The U.S. Department of Agriculture (USDA) does not endorse any products, services,
or organizations.**

Note to Parents and Teachers

The Healthy Eating with MyPyramid set supports national science standards related
to nutrition and physical health. This book describes and illustrates ways for kids to be
active. The images support early readers in understanding the text. The repetition of
words and phrases helps early readers learn new words. This book also introduces early
readers to subject-specific vocabulary words, which are defined in the Glossary section.
Early readers may need assistance to read some words and to use the Table of Contents,
Glossary, Read More, Internet Sites, and Index sections of the book.

Printed in the United States of America in North Mankato, Minnesota.
022011
006057R

Table of Contents

Being Active

Being active is about
playing, moving your body,
and exercising.
How have you
been active today?

Smile! Being active
makes you feel happy
and good about yourself.
It can help you stay
at a healthy weight.

MyPyramid for Kids

Being active is
a part of MyPyramid.
MyPyramid is a tool
to help you eat right
and stay in shape.

MyPyramid For Kids
Eat Right. Exercise. Have Fun.

To learn more about
healthy eating and staying
active, go to this web site:
www.MyPyramid.gov/kids
Ask an adult for help.

Kids need to be active

at least 60 minutes every day.

Try to move more

and sit less!

Get Moving

Being active is easy and fun.

Play tag with your friends.

Who will you catch first?

Dribble, pass, shoot.

Play basketball after school.

Get your heart pumping.

Time to walk the dog.

Take a jog

around the park.

Pedal hard to get moving.

Go for a bike ride

with your family.

Being active helps keep
you healthy and fit.
How do you like to be active?

Ways to Be Active

Kids need to exercise and be active at least 60 minutes every day. Here are some ideas to get you moving. What other ways can you be active?

swimming

jumping rope

in-line skating

dancing

soccer

running

riding bike

playing catch

Glossary

exercise—to make your body work hard through activities like sports; exercising helps keep you fit and healthy.

healthy—being fit and well

MyPyramid—a food plan that helps kids make healthy food choices and reminds kids to be active; MyPyramid was created by the U.S. Department of Agriculture.

Read More

Rockwell, Lizzy. *The Busy Body Book: A Kid's Guide to Fitness.* New York: Crown, 2004.

Salzmann, Mary Elizabeth. *Being Active.* Healthy Habits. Edina, Minn.: Abdo, 2004.

Spilsbury, Louise. *Why Should I Get Off the Couch?: and Other Questions About Health and Exercise.* Heinemann Infosearch. Chicago: Heinemann, 2003.

Index

Word Count: 140
Grade: 1
Early-Intervention Level: 14

Internet Sites

FactHound offers a safe, fun way to find Internet sites related to this book. All of the sites on FactHound have been researched by our staff.

Here's how:

1. Visit *www.facthound.com*

2. Type in this special code **0736853685** for age-appropriate sites. Or enter a search word related to this book for a more general search.

3. Click on the **Fetch It** button.

FactHound will fetch the best sites for you!